QUOTES
—— *of* ——
PRAISE

Nancy Winningham

authorHOUSE®

AuthorHouse™
1663 Liberty Drive
Bloomington, IN 47403
www.authorhouse.com
Phone: 1 (800) 839-8640

Published by AuthorHouse 03/17/2016

ISBN: 978-1-5049-7844-6 (sc)
ISBN: 978-1-5049-7843-9 (e)

Library of Congress Control Number: 2016902365

Print information available on the last page.

Quotes of Praise

Nancy Winningham

ACKNOWLEDGEMENTS

There are numerous individuals who have devoted time, encouragement, and love during the improvement of this magnificent accomplishment and they are praiseworthy of the acknowledgement. First, I will acknowledge God, who has given me the words, insight, strength, and knowledge to begin and complete this book, without God it would have been impossible for me to consolidate a book such as this. These Quotes will allow all who reads them to administer praise and will relate these quotes toward their everyday life experiences. Due to the different test of greatness that has come upon me during my journey I was still able to provide an eminence of moving quotes because of these individuals. Their assurance in me forms the inspiration within my soul to deliver these moving words to you. I will forever be grateful for all the suggestions and support that was given to me while being able to accept corrective criticism. Thank you to all of my wonderful family and friends for your support.

DEDICATION

There are some astonishing people I would love to dedicate this book to:

To my marvelous husband Fredrick Wayne Hurt Winningham, who continues to be my motivator, thoughtful, helpful, truthful, honorable, and devoted since the day we met. I love you my Sweetie Pie, thank you for loving me, and thank you for being the inspiration that I always need.

To our son Gregory, who always shows himself strong despite any and all circumstances. You've always encouraged me to achieve greater and you are an example of a great father. Thank you and God's continued protection and abundance of favor over your life.

To our son Antonio, who is the most humorous of them all. You continue to strive toward higher achievements and for this may God continue to grace you with ongoing grace and favor upon your life.

To our youngest son Thomias, who shows an enormous of powerful strength, courage, and love for all. Thank you for being so amazing and God's continued Blessings upon your life.

To all of my brothers, sisters, additional family, friends, and for those who showed their support in helping to make this creation achievable, for all I am grateful.

A special thank you to all the people who God placed into my life both good and bad, due to them my life preserved power.

"When in doubt pray it out!"

~Nancy Winningham~

"When you don't know it won't show."

~Nancy Winningham~

"My past uproots my future."

~Nancy Winningham~

"A positive reaction to the distraction
allows one to be proactive."

~Nancy Winningham~

"It is not hard to praise God."

~Nancy Winningham~

"My soul is my closet to conscientiousness."

~Nancy Winningham~

"I have to go through some breakups before
I can get to my break through."

~Nancy Winningham~

"The way a child learns is a reflection on he's taught."

~Nancy Winningham~

"Start recognizing who you are to
get to where you need to be."

~Nancy Winningham~

"God's love filters my inner being."

~Nancy Winningham~

"It is not how much money you make it is what you do with it to make it grow."

~Nancy Winningham~

"I receive because I believe."

~Nancy Winningham~

"The essay of my life is summarized with a quote."

~Nancy Winningham~

"God's grace finishes my race."

~Nancy Winningham~

"Negativity is not part of the priority."

~Nancy Winningham~

"Know what you had to do to get to where you are."

~Nancy Winningham~

"One would not understand my right now
because it was my back then that got me here."

~Nancy Winningham~

"There is no need for stressing during a lesson,
instead remember God is blessing."

~Nancy Winningham~

"Hope is like a knotted rope but when you
let go it does not seem easy to cope."

~Nancy Winningham~

"Dreams are thoughts waiting for action to take place."

~Nancy Winningham~

"Dreams are highlights to what is to come."

~Nancy Winningham~

"One of the best messages I've received is from the mess that I have been delivered from."

~Nancy Winningham~

"What is happening to you is meant to help you."

~Nancy Winningham~

"Small minded people have small minded ideas."

~Nancy Winningham~

"Productivity is my specialty."

~Nancy Winningham~

"I thank God for the correction, I thank God for the direction, and I thank God for his protection."

~Nancy Winningham~

"An obstacle is needed to get to where you need to be."

~Nancy Winningham~

"When there is pressure there is pain,
during the pressure and pain is praise."

~Nancy Winningham~

"God I thank you for the experience and
I thank you for the deliverance."

~Nancy Winningham~

"I excel because my God always prevails."

~Nancy Winningham~

"Pain is a poisonous position."

~Nancy Winningham~

"God will turn one's disability into a capability to maintain stability."

~Nancy Winningham~

"There is no pause in my praise."

~Nancy Winningham~

"Not knowing slows down ones process of growing."

~Nancy Winningham~

"God will turn your struggle into strength."

~Nancy Winningham~

"Don't set limitations, set expectations."

~Nancy Winningham~

"The flight to my circumstance becomes my reality."

~Nancy Winningham~

"God works for my good like no other would."

~Nancy Winningham~

"God reminds me of a book, He is the beginning, middle, and the end."

~Nancy Winningham~

"When God provides you an opportunity don't allow others to make it an option to disrespect you."

~Nancy Winningham~

"There is praise throughout my pain."

~Nancy Winningham~

"I refuse to be your part-time or down
time when I am your full-time."

~Nancy Winningham~

"If you are not on time I don't have the time."

~Nancy Winningham~

"Gratitude brings the greatness within you."

~Nancy Winningham~

"To enhance you have to be open to opportunities."

~Nancy Winningham~

"Today's triumph tomorrow's testimony."

~Nancy Winningham~

"When man exempts God accepts."

~Nancy Winningham~

"God allows me to go through the storm to enter into the sunshine."

~Nancy Winningham~

"Today is a day that yesterday is not, it's a new day with new beginnings."

~Nancy Winningham~

"When life throws you a curve ball, know
that your home run is on the way."

~Nancy Winningham~

"Ignorance does not bring happiness."

~Nancy Winningham~

"Expect the greater by embracing your hater."

~Nancy Winningham~

"Don't be bitter because God is sweet."

~Nancy Winningham~

"God reminds me of an American Express card, you can't leave home without Him."

~Nancy Winningham~

"God reminds me of a spotlight,
He shines right on me."

~Nancy Winningham~

"God will make up for your mess ups."

~Nancy Winningham~

"A negative attitude decreases your gratitude."

~Nancy Winningham~

"God is able to the unstable, disabled, and capable."

~Nancy Winningham~

"God will take action throughout all distractions."

~Nancy Winningham~

"Determination is like walking up a step less ladder."

~Nancy Winningham~

"A lack of communication can show less dedication."

~Nancy Winningham~

"God transcends, transforms, and reforms."

~Nancy Winningham~

"As God is resolving I am revolving."

~Nancy Winningham~

"God reminds me of a mail carrier He is a deliverer."

~Nancy Winningham~

"Don't discuss your story during your road trip,
tell it once you reach your destination."

~Nancy Winningham~

"God will transform your past position
into a reformed present."

~Nancy Winningham~

"God interviews the qualified and hires the called."

~Nancy Winningham~

"Do you but don't do me!"

~Nancy Winningham~

"Accept it and correct it."

~Nancy Winningham~

"The lights are on when you're figuring it out,
the lights go out when you've concluded."

~Nancy Winningham

"It is not where you are, it is where you are going."

~Nancy Winningham~

"Ultimate healing is an awesome feeling."

~Nancy Winningham~

"I strive because I thrive."

~Nancy Winningham~

"God teaches His students on an individual basis"

~Nancy Winningham~

"God's power uplifts my praise."

~Nancy Winningham~

"A battle may make my life rattle but at the end of the day I am holding on like a horse's saddle."

~Nancy Winningham~

"Inconsistent people is like a seed
without nourishment."

~Nancy Winningham~

"Life reminds me of a washing machine cycle; sometimes I have to go through the wash, the rinse, spin, and lastly the dry."

~Nancy Winningham~

"My life is like looking at the film before it's released."

~Nancy Winningham~

"Sometimes life is like a ripped up, balled up piece of paper, just open it, put the pieces together, and re-write your story."

~Nancy Winningham~

"Make like the sun and shine."

~Nancy Winningham~

"Lord when I am in need of a monetary blessing, Lord make a way so I can pay."

~Nancy Winningham~

"It is a deadline to every distraction."

~Nancy Winningham~

"I have to go through it to thank God for it."

~Nancy Winningham~

"No matter what you're going through
God is working for you."

~Nancy Winningham~

"There is no failure in my future."

~Nancy Winningham~

"Living for the right now will not get
you where you need to be."

~Nancy Winningham~

"Don't be vengeful when the expectancy is victory."

~Nancy Winningham~

"Slow in the mind brings slow reactions."

~Nancy Winningham~

"There is no win in sin."

~Nancy Winningham~

"Stupidity has no validity."

~Nancy Winningham~

"Life is to love, live, and let go."

~Nancy Winningham~

"You have to love the life you live to let
go of what's not nourishing it."

~Nancy Winningham~

"You don't get blessed without a test."

~Nancy Winningham~

"What happens to us is happening to help us."

~Nancy Winningham~

"Know what you need to do to
live the life you deserve."

~Nancy Winningham~

"Be the answer to your questions."

~Nancy Winningham~

"Lord thank you for what I am going through and thank you for what you are going to do."

~Nancy Winningham~

"When you put nothing into life you
will receive insufficient funds."

~Nancy Winningham~

"Be a chain breaker not a chain maker."

~Nancy Winningham~

"The more the distractions the more the infractions."

~Nancy Winningham~

"When you want to go far you will
shine like the star that you are."

~Nancy Winningham~

"Don't get stuck on people because you will lose focus on your purpose."

~Nancy Winningham~

"A man that says a little thinks a lot."

~Nancy Winningham~

"Be a warrior not a worrier."

~Nancy Winningham~

"Losing does not mean you've lost the battle
it means you have begun the fight."

~Nancy Winningham~

"God never rejects me, neglects me,
instead He completes me."

~Nancy Winningham~

"Looking back from how far God has
brought you serves a great purpose."

~Nancy Winningham~

"The haters and the naysayers make you greater."

~Nancy Winningham~

"God's love is perpetual."

~Nancy Winningham~

"You can't get yourself worked up over something that's already messed up."

~Nancy Winningham~

"I'm a warrior not a worrier."

~Nancy Winningham~

"Life is like a walk in the park you show determination even when it's dark."

~Nancy Winningham~

"I will outshine darkness."

~Nancy Winningham~

"A way out is God's way of looking out."

~Nancy Winningham~

"The best route to go is letting it go."

~Nancy Winningham~

"Incompetency is not a good policy."

~Nancy Winningham~

"What you learn today you will know tomorrow."

~Nancy Winningham~

"As long as you are involved with weak minded people you are a target for punishment."

~Nancy Winningham~

"You cannot drive down two roads because you may be bound for an accident, if it is not God's way you are going the wrong way."

~Nancy Winningham~

"When there is a trial and a test it shows that God knows best."

~Nancy Winningham~

"God is the King of Glory who
writes my marvelous story."

~Nancy Winningham~

"Those who don't know refuse to let it go."

~Nancy Winningham~

"The accidents in my life becomes opportunities."

~Nancy Winningham~

"Everyone will not be excited about the positive resolution to your conclusion."

~Nancy Winningham~

"People who have lost their way will come back once they find their how."

~Nancy Winningham~

"God bless the stress."

~Nancy Winningham~

"Pain is for a purpose."

~Nancy Winningham~

"While the enemy is mad God is glad."

~Nancy Winningham~

"Mute those who don't deserve the play button."

~Nancy Winningham~

"When you believe in your thank you,
you are walking in your gratitude."

~Nancy Winningham~

"Live for today for a marvelous tomorrow."

~Nancy Winningham~

"God will turn your tragedy into a triumph."

~Nancy Winningham~

"The same thing you are complaining
about somebody is praying about."

~Nancy Winningham~

"It is nice to be compassionate about one's passion."

~Nancy Winningham~

"Thank you God for the look back and
thank you God for not going back."

~Nancy Winningham~

"Be thankful for it all despite it all."

~Nancy Winningham~

"Thankfulness shows fulfillment."

~Nancy Winningham~

"Talk less and do more."

~Nancy Winningham~

"Thank you God for another day, you didn't
have to do it but you did it anyway."

~Nancy Winningham~

"With every opposition is an opportunity."

~Nancy Winningham~

"Thank you Lord for shining through
me so others may see."

~Nancy Winningham~

"If you don't expect more you will receive less."

~Nancy Winningham~

"The Lord gives you confirmation on
how to reach your destination."

~Nancy Winningham~

"A hater is a procrastinator."

~Nancy Winningham~

"A shut down is not a shut up."

~Nancy Winningham~

"Hanging out with eagles causes you
to soar toward higher heights."

~Nancy Winningham~

"I am thankful that God is the CEO
of the company that I work for."

Benefit Package Includes:

1. He pays right on time.

2. He has an open door policy.

3. He is an outstanding gift giver.

4. He provides increase.

5. He never does any layoffs.

~Nancy Winningham~

"If you are not being hated on you
don't have nothing going on."

~Nancy Winningham~

"God is working for the good like no other would."

~Nancy Winningham~

"Trust is a must."

~Nancy Winningham~

"While the enemy is mad God is glad."

~Nancy Winningham~

"Stop throwing shade on someone else's parade
because yours does not have a marching band."

~Nancy Winningham~

"What's meant is going to show, what is not will go."

~Nancy Winningham~

"You have to let one know by letting them go."

~Nancy Winningham~

"An unhappy space equals an unhappy face."

~Nancy Winningham~

"Stop pacifying the problem and
begin acting on the solution."

~Nancy Winningham~

"One needs to feel validated and not illuminated."

~Nancy Winningham~

"Religion is a tool box that's used to assist
with directing and correcting."

~Nancy Winningham~

"Spirituality is a connection that needs no correction."

~Nancy Winningham~

"I will dance while I have a chance
despite the circumstance."

~Nancy Winningham~

"Don't allow someone else's distraction to
interfere with your positive reaction."

~Nancy Winningham~

"I've got it because God's got it."

~Nancy Winningham~

TAP Into Your Spiritual Base

Thankfulness for everything and everyone, the good, bad, and the ugly.

Act on it! Stay in tune.

Practice your Spiritual Base Daily.

Printed in the United States
By Bookmasters